A LIGHT IN EVERY DIRECTION

A LIGHT IN EVERY DIRECTION

NITU RAMCHANDANI

PAPER TOWNS
PUBLISHERS

PAPER TOWNS
PUBLISHERS

First published by
Papertowns Publishers
72, Vishwanath Dham Colony,
Niwaru Road, Jhotwara,
Jaipur, 302012

A Light in Every Direction

ISBN Print Book - 978-93-87131-98-9

Cover Design by Amit Ramchandani
Email: amitr18x@gmail.com

Dedicated to my mom, dearest love of my life.

ACKNOWLEDGEMENTS

Big big thank you Rishabh Jain and Yagya Dutta for always staying by my side. And to my biggest supporters and well-wishers, my mom, my dad and Amit Ramchandani, a big thank you!

Thanks to all the beautiful readers who chose to read my book. And a very big thank you to my dear principal mam (Sanjeevani Dobhal) from Helen Keller Blind School, for always loving me unconditionally.

Thank you everyone at the Bookoholics and my publisher, for making my dreams come true by publishing my books. Thank you so much! You make me so happy.

CONTENTS

ACCEPTANCE

Happy realizations
Welcome beauty and acceptance
In a life of hardships
Challenge your limits of tolerance

The broader is perspective
The more we are flexible
The more we accept
The more we ought to be humble

How acceptance heals you gradually

We people keep facing problems in our day-to-day life and feel helpless sometimes. These problems do have solutions. We all just need to realize that a problem is a chance for us to expand our creative sense. And this will ultimately help us to realize that our problems are not too big and the majority of them can vanish from our life if we just choose to see at the bright side of the things.

The first time I won the battle, which I was fighting against depression, anxiety and insomnia, it was by simply looking at the bright side of every little thing. My reaction when I first came to know that depression hit me and that I had to start taking medicines for the elimination of this mental disorder was like 'at least something new happened in my life'. And I think this is the reason why I was able to accept it and win bit by bit.

The thing is most of the times we keep thinking about our problems rather than focusing on solutions which makes even the simpler issues seem too big and complicated. We can always try shifting our perspective beyond the actual scene. This will not only help us in battling with things but also discover something new that the world might have never seen before. And while we try to overcome the challenges life keeps presenting before us, we can always choose to stay flexible and kind with ourselves. By observing people around, we come to know that everyone is already fighting their own battles, so rather than being strict, one can always learn to be humble and compassionate towards others to minimize the damage that is caused due to certain hardships.

Messages to conclude:-

1. Turn anger to humility, attitude to nature, negativity to the bright side, arguments to opinions, problems to challenges and challenges to opportunities for growth. We must understand that we are always able enough to give ourselves a chance to change our perspective and view things differently than what they seem to be.

2. What can be changed, change it; accept the rest and move on. Don't take life too seriously. Have fun while advancing along the path of your goals.

3. The broader our perspective, the more chances we get to understand the opportunities life keeps giving us to get closer to our dreams.

4. Instead of searching differences in each other, we must explore our similarities together because that opens more doors for love and acceptance in our lives.

STRUGGLES

Adjust the sail
Like a brave warrior
Physical or mental pain
Be a resilient survivor

Tears, blood or sweat
Bear it all with a smile
Fight with anxiety and demons
Helps to recover from turmoil

Series of struggles that I conquered with a smile

From school and college times, I've been continuously struggling to fight my battles. I've got operation of teeth (also put braces for treatment of uneven alignment), scar mark (above my left eyebrow) and eyes (for treatment of myopia) done. Also, whenever I used to have my exams in school and college, I would get a cough and cold. I've always struggled to win different battles as I've seen a series of events unfolding in my life one after another. When I was pursuing engineering, I got an offer from HSBC after getting placed by clearing all the rounds of interviews. Unfortunately, as the requirements in the company were frozen (seats were full) at that time, I could not join it. I then joined a dance class for a year, and one night I also wrote a poem (out of happiness) to express my emotions, but I could not continue the class as I started to show symptoms of insomnia (my family was worried about me). In 2017, I joined a college for pursuing MBA (went there for 3-4 months) but did not feel like continuing it due to some personal problems. In March 2018, depression hit me, and it was cured till January 2020.

In 2019, I worked in a BPO company (call centre) recommended by a senior friend from college. While working there, I was again recommended by a friend to join another company, i.e. Amazon. I cleared all the rounds, got selected, but did not join as I wanted to do some social work so that I could help people in need. So then, I went to become an English teacher in a blind school and taught for free. Simultaneously, I also worked on writing my first poetry book "Infinite Delight" in the same year. In 2016, I had written my first poem. Then after two years, in 2018, I realized it through a friend that I wrote really good poetry. So, I again started writing and now dreamt of becoming an excellent poet, writer and author. It was April 2020 when the same mental disorders of depression, anxiety and insomnia again hit me (relapse happened). Still, with my friends and family by my side, I have complete faith that again I'll be able to win my battle against it and also as I've found my root cause, I think it will be easier to tackle it this time. Now I've started to accept things in a much more welcoming way than before. And again I've also started dancing to work on my expressions and to brush up my dancing skills. Through all these years of hardships, I got to learn many life lessons which have ultimately made me emotionally and mentally strong.

Messages to conclude:-

1. Be in a healthy competition with the person you were yesterday. Be better today.

2. Live away from all your habits for a day and see where you stand in life.

3. We all fight two battles, one with ourselves and one with the outer world. Hence, we need to be kind to everyone, including us.

4. Be unstoppable, undefeatable, unbelievable.

5. Happy plus calm is a kind of superpower that can make you achieve the biggest of dreams and help you fight the biggest of battles.

6. Don't let the storms in your life break you, let them make you.

HOPE

Be your own light
Find strength in the spark
Carry love and faith
As weapons in the dark

Darkness shall leave
Light shall enter
Live free from fear
With no single tear

When I discovered hope in my life

There used to be days in my depression mode when I used to cry from morning till evening in my room. I cried so much that I could not breathe. Nobody came to know about it. I used to keep thinking about the reason but could not figure out what made me cry so much. Only later, I discovered that in my case, small reasons added up to grow into some significant fear/doubt, and the heaviness made me cry before I could learn to express things. I think it's essential that our generation must be allowed to express their thoughts openly. When one day, after I was tired of crying, some spark in me made me get up from my bed and then I had some water, and then I sat and thought that I had to get up for myself and that's when I think I discovered hope. Later, I also wrote a poem on hope. From then on, I have always been explaining to myself that our life is our responsibility, and only we can understand our battles better than anyone else. We can take support from others, but we can also learn to be self-reliant. There is infinite hope (little voice/little spark) in our hearts which can always help us in our journey for every little thing if we just keep calm and show some patience while our souls guide us along the way. We must observe ourselves and listen to that little voice because it knows what is best for us.

What hope looks like:-

- To discover possibilities where you find none
- The little flame inside you says that goodwill shall unite everyone one day
- You are aware that you carry infinite love in your heart and never let that light/spark of love dim away
- You find strength in the spark lighting in your heart

- You can be your own light
- To keep faith in your ability to make things right when sometimes they don't go smooth
- To keep faith in your inner power to cope up when the road/path of life seems a bit difficult
- To smile in difficult times and know that smiling Earth shall strive with every effort to survive
- You are gentle with yourself and allow the light to fill in the wounds

Messages to conclude:-

1. When you feel like giving up, hope whispers just once more, and that once more always makes you extraordinary.

2. Ever felt lost? Have faith; what's meant for you will come back to make you rise.

3. Be your own master, be your own teacher, be your own trainer, be your own light, be your own hero.

4. Hope is instinct reasoned with intuition. Always keep hope alive.

5. Discover the possibilities where you find none. See problems as opportunities to push your creative boundaries.

6. Things become fine when you choose to shine. Everything works in your favour as long as you allow it to; let a strong purpose guide you, visualize a big picture, let it pull you forward, let it drive you to achieve heights in life. The more you dedicate to your art, the more it will return you.

HEALING

Forget and forgive
Make new beginnings
To heal the hurt
Simply count your blessings

Fill wounds with light
Always choose to rise
In the adverse times
Endurance makes one wise

How healing helps in recovery

Healing is a process in which we allow ourselves to feel things (both good and bad) and learn to let the painful moments go. It is rightly said that wounds do heal and fade away with time. We just have to be more self-aware to know that acceptance and faith collectively have the power to heal us. We can always choose to rise by making ourselves feel blessed intentionally. This helps us choose a good mood which ultimately helps us in the nourishment of our body, mind and soul. Acceptance of circumstances while living fully in the present makes our journey extremely beautiful as we can experience and enjoy life as it comes.

Forgive yourself for your past mistakes as quickly as you forgive everyone else. Try to understand your feelings and emotions so that you can know where to make changes. When you observe yourself, it becomes easy to heal and recover as you become more aware of the things that genuinely affect you and when once you are clear about your concerns, you begin to understand what to accept and what not. When you start to heal, you'll begin to find happiness in small moments. Learn lessons from every challenge you face so that you can grow through your experiences and add meaning to your life.

Every day, we can work on ourselves, bit by bit, to replace negative thoughts with positive ones. Also, this way, we can give out positive energy and raise our vibrations. One can always try different methods to cheer oneself up like eating something healthy, go for a walk in nature to take fresh air or talk to a friend to figure things out, listen to some inspirational songs etc. Reach out for help whenever needed. Simply sharing your feelings with someone can help you find different ways to cope and to spread love and hope, which ultimately enables you to heal your spirit. Smile often that you are blessed enough to visualize a dream and make it come true. Make a list of tasks that you have to perform throughout the day/week so that you can work more efficiently. When we are busy with our goals, there is not much time left for negativity. Help yourself in creating the kind of life you dream to live.

Messages to conclude:-

1. Repeating these sentences helps a lot in life :
   - I don't focus on the past.
   - I live in the present.
   - Healing takes time.
   - I feel happy and fresh.

2. You are what you are today because of all the things you went through. Have no grudges, no regrets, no complaints and no demands.

3. Fight the beast of chaos in your mind through endurance. Only that shall give you clarity (to identify good) and the real power of self-control and inner strength.

4. Whenever things get too hard, simply start counting your blessings, and you'll see that this technique always helps to heal the hurt.

GRACE

Like warmth in winter
Our progress we embrace
Moments taking the breath away
Bring growth and grace

The power lies within you
Remember what you gain
Hold the balance
For sweet is pleasure after pain

When grace added beauty in life

Growing relationships with people has always been graceful in my case. When it comes to friendship, I love to nurture the relation gracefully. Whenever I meet a new person, slowly I understand him/her and then open up gradually to form a strong bond. Be it a friend or a family member, it takes time to build a good relation, a kind of relation in which trust and faith are mutual so that one can serve their partner in all the supportive ways. Whenever you make new friends, you share all your interests with them and then life is completely adventurous with them. Life gives a fair chance to everyone to build relationships with people who we think deserve to be with us. When it comes to family, they are always there for you to help you grow in incredible ways. Their support is endless and they love you unconditionally. You can flourish effortlessly with the blessings of your family. Apart from family, friends too provide great support so that we can learn new things together. In initial stages, when we meet a person, everything is new, slowly we discover things about each other and then finally we end up sharing every little thing with this new friend.

Not only in growing relationships, but grace can also be observed in every little thing that grows with poise, beauty and love. Examples of graceful moments include growing of a flower from its bud, growing of a little child from a baby to a 6-7 years old boy/girl, growth process of a butterfly, formation of rainbows, the way two individuals love each other upto infinity, the way a dancer dances effortlessly, the way an individual carries himself/herself etc.

Messages to conclude :-

1. Let there be no hurry, no worry, no gloom, just bloom.

2. Laugh like a king, grow like a flower, shine bright like a diamond, and stay flexible like a dancer.

3. In hard times, have more faith, believe more in you, be extra kind towards yourself, hold onto your strengths and stay flexible to provide yourself the necessary support needed to heal your heart and soul.

HAPPINESS

Overwhelmed with gratitude
Filled with love
When something resonates
It feels like true love

New ideas bring joy
Ecstasy and satisfaction
To spread good vibes
Be your best version

What is happiness?
How do you describe happy moments?

Happiness is when:-

- You get to share smiles with someone (It multiplies the madness)
- You enjoy little moments to their fullest
- You feel overwhelmed with gratitude
- You are surprised with a good news
- You see a smile on your parents' face (especially when you are the reason behind that smile)
- You can have simple yet meaningful conversations with your special friends
- You get to buy gifts for making someone feel special
- You can celebrate festivals with your cousins
- You can share your ideas with the world (new ideas bring joy)
- You get tears of joy in your eyes (especially when you've put the required amount of hard work to achieve a goal/dream)
- You can accomplish small tasks (happiness hormones are released)
- You are full of hope and optimism
- You can face and win a challenge
- You allow yourselves to follow your heart
- You are someone's inspiration
- You can perform random acts of kindness

Messages to conclude:-

1. The actions you take every moment are creating your story. Make sure you live your best life. (You only live once)

2. Love is such a superpower which makes you do things that otherwise seem to be impossible.

3. We can always make ourselves best for all those people we have in our lives.

4. Work hard and let happiness be the reward you give to yourselves every single day.

5. Live in the present, not past, not future; focus at your present version, focus on positive, focus on the bright side and see how you shall achieve heights and highest happiness in your life.

6. Understand the difference between the two situations: you are happy, so you enjoy your work, or you work, and then you become happy. Work for permanent happiness rather than temporary solutions.

7. The best feeling in the world is when you get tears of joy in your eyes. Work hard for the kind of feeling that gives you joy and goosebumps.

8. Don't stress over anything in life because it only takes your happiness away from you. Feel and do things with your heart immersed in them. Little changes bring huge improvement with time.

GRATITUDE

For all the smiles
Lovely friends and family
For sunshine and every new day —
Rich blessings keep troubles away

For all the lessons
Learning from mistakes
For energy and optimism
Be thankful for all the enthusiasm

Gratitude –
The most beautiful chapter of life

At random, one day, when I started to count my blessings, I found myself speechless because of gratitude. I was surprised at the fact that sometimes we forget how blessed we are. We are blessed even beyond what we can imagine.

Whenever I find myself even in a small fight with someone, I always think that at least I have that someone to fight with. And this very thought keeps making me realize how blessed I am and that there is no point in holding a grudge against someone. The more we count our blessings, the more content we become. Every new day is a blessing, so we must be grateful for every little thing in life.

Be grateful for your loved ones and for all the smiles you share with them. Be grateful for all the people you meet in your life. Be grateful for the people who support you in your journey and who help you in achieving your dreams. Be grateful for all the opportunities life keeps presenting in front of you. Be grateful for all the lessons you get to learn in life. Be grateful for your mind, body, heart and soul. Be grateful for Earth, nature and your surroundings that allow you to grow.

Messages to conclude:-

1. I have nothing to lose today still I am grateful for what I have. (A note to self)

2. Forgive yourself for your past mistakes. Be thankful for all the lessons and learning from those mistakes. Always look up and keep moving forward in life.

3. Be grateful for your heart, be grateful that you are alive and breathing, be thankful for sunshine and every new day, be thankful for energy and optimism, be grateful for all the enthusiasm in your life.

4. Wake up with enthusiasm and gratefulness every single day to go on a journey to perform your best till you have to go to bed because every new day is a blessing that you're alive and breathing. And when given a chance/ opportunity, choose to rise by taking the responsibility.

WISDOM

Absorb and observe
Your feelings and emotions
Make yourself aware —
Choose wisdom and patience

When each tear says
Let me be a tear of joy
When karma seems like wisdom —
Life is truly meant to enjoy

How wisdom is a never-ending process of learning

I believe in the concept of feel, explore and discover, which means finding new things upon we have explored about certain interests or after we have felt them with all our heart. Feeling things expands our perspective. Exploring stuff out of curiosity also helps to broaden our viewpoint, which ultimately helps us in acquiring wisdom.

We must review our behaviour consistently and give ourselves time to absorb things and learn from every experience. We can always observe our emotions to keep a regular check on our thoughts. Once we start understanding our thought pattern, we can explore our deeper inner-selves to make the most out of the only life that we've got.

When we begin to understand the situations that genuinely affect or touch us, we can make the right decisions for ourselves. This gives us a sense of purpose in life, which ultimately helps us to take every action wisely.

Messages to conclude:-

1. Deep within the Earth, we find treasures which become useful elements due to pressure. Similarly, deep within our heart are treasures we can find if only we allow ourselves to feel.

2. What we experience every little moment is altogether different for different individuals. Therefore, there is no point in comparing one person with another. Our journeys are different. One must focus on investing in oneself.

3. Take some time to self-introspect because that would be one of the best and most significant investments you could ever make. Explore your inner self to discover the most mysterious secrets that your heart holds.

4. The decisions that we make in life affect our dreams, goals and purpose. They help us decide our passion; they ensure that we move ahead in the right direction. Hence, the power of choice is such that it can give all of us beautiful lives but only when we make those choices wisely.

5. Sometimes, we should just sit silently and review our behaviour. Also, we should keep a regular check on our thoughts and activities so that we can observe whether we are going in the right direction or not. We must reflect upon how things are going and must give ourselves time to absorb them.

6. We must keep revising our values, virtues and acquired lessons thoroughly so that we can readily accept the challenge of what lies in front of us.

7. Time is precious; use it wisely.

8. Whenever you have to make some changes in your life (or lifestyle habits), remember you need to be extra patient with yourself because good things always take time to incorporate/absorb.

LEARNING

Learn from nature
What life has to offer —
Never stop learning
Because life will never cease teaching

Discard old beliefs
To adopt new values —
See problems as opportunities
And push your creative boundaries

How being open-minded helps to accept new ideas/opinions

I have learnt a crucial lesson that we can learn lessons from anything and everything in life. Life has a very fantastic way to teach us lessons through different experiences. Our thoughts develop our mindset which ultimately defines our actions. Our actions are a result of our learning and based on the wisdom that we acquire in our journey. We can learn lessons from good experiences by analyzing that how things happen when they go well. We can learn from bad experiences too by questioning ourselves that what might have gone wrong that we were unable to achieve the desired outcome and then we can improve accordingly. We can learn lessons from our mistakes by observing ourselves while carrying out our tasks so that we do not repeat the same mistake the next time we perform a same kind of activity. Failures are nothing but a way of life to teach us important lessons so that we can better ourselves with every mistake. Using our learning in wise ways not only helps us to become great at our work but also to become a better person in life. When we perform our job by being our best version, we become more efficient at performing it wholeheartedly. Apart from learning from our experiences, failures and mistakes, we can also learn lessons by observing nature and our surroundings. The way things in nature grow gracefully; watching them, we can learn incredible lessons. We can understand this wonderful lesson from nature that we should always remain calm during inevitable storms in life because these storms come only to challenge us and to test whether we are patient enough to focus on our growth or not. Suppose one needs to have great strength to bear tough challenges in life, in that case, first, one must practice staying calm, peaceful, happy and optimistic in every kind of situation believing that whatever happens, happens for our good only. If not today, at least tomorrow, our hard work will add value and meaning to our lives as we simultaneously get a chance to work on our patience and growth every time we choose diligence.

Messages to conclude:-

1. Challenges are nothing but some kind of tests in life so that we can discover about our hidden powers that otherwise lie/remain dormant.

2. Isolation stimulates the creative mind. You can always try some mental exercise for activities which involve creativity of mind.

3. Embrace the good, endure through the bad. Learn not only from bad experiences but from good too.

4. Repeating this sentence helps a lot :
   I will always be eager for learning as I love to take a lesson before the blessing.

5. Our battles don't come to break us; instead, they arrive so that we can prepare ourselves for new opportunities; they come to make us learn the art of life.

6. Passion makes you feel alive, like having an adventure. It fills you with enthusiasm. It is an intense emotion that makes you work with determination. Know and follow your passion.

7. While you advance along your journey of experiences, don't forget to make memories and build good relationships with your loved and special ones.

8. When there's some emotion inside you, it's always trying to teach you something. Keep focusing on the lessons life teaches you and it will help you grow beyond limits. Trust the process of growth. Accept life as it unfolds every moment. Acceptance of circumstances heals you gradually.

9. More than looking for the number of problems, look for possibilities and solutions and see how it affects your growth in a positive manner. The more you focus on solutions, the more they increase/multiply.

10. Life teaches a lot many lessons only when we know how to observe and learn.

11. Don't be too strict with yourself; you are only human; you are only learning; it's okay to take time to evolve in your flexible ways.

THOUGHTS

Allow the best thoughts
To nurture your mind
In difficult times
Be kind to your mind

Thoughts reap actions
For they are powerful —
Give out positive energy
For it makes life beautiful

4. The way your thoughts hold power to bring you a beautiful life

I believe that the thoughts that we think through our conscious mind play a crucial role in our lives. What we think influences directly how we feel, which ultimately influences our energy. When we think empowering thoughts, it not only helps us to take virtuous actions but also to change our mood to a more positive one. When we allow our minds to always look at the bright side of the things, it reflects in our behaviour. When we are aware of what we allow to enter our minds, we can take control of our actions wisely. Following points can be kept in mind while we learn to think better and more pleasant thoughts:-

1. Life didn't come with a reference book on how to live, but it has gifted us experiences, opportunities and blessings. So we can always take some time to question our actions to enhance our understanding of moments/situations.

2. Take time to reflect upon your analysis/perception of things so that you can keep refining your behaviour towards handling them in better ways.

3. Take a little pause before you react. Take time to think and change your response towards circumstances that challenge you and your beliefs. Most of the times, you'll be able to respond in a better and a more polite way which will eventually help you live a more peaceful life.

4. Whenever you don't feel good, at that moment, remind yourself of all the good things you are blessed with in your life. Remind yourself of all the values/morals that you follow so that you can hold on to your strengths

(motivate yourself) and realize that you do have immense inner power to fight your battles.

5. Feed good words to your mind to awaken your spirit to spread more good vibes and greater energy.

I have observed that practising these points regularly can help us to remind us that the power required to change our thought pattern already lies within us. Once we realize this fact, we all can become more optimistic and eventually better individuals.

Messages to conclude:-

1. We can always try using different kind of formulas for different situations (for a peaceful life) :-
   Patience + Acceptance (Healing) = Recovery
   Worth + Growth = Basic need
   Strength + Hope + Confidence = Revive
   Harmony + Balance = Unity (sync)
   Calm + Love = Superpower
   Sorrow + A child's smile = Happy feeling
   Balance + Happiness + Sadness + Family + Friend + Food = Life

2. In a negative situation, make yourself feel good by thinking positive thoughts and keep chasing more of such positive thoughts till they make you win.

3. In every situation, we have two choices, either to rise by being positive or to choose the first choice.

4. Everything you think can be replaced with something better. It is scary how fast life is changing, but this is how you evolve.

5. Let yourself be a sum of all your good and empowering thoughts rather than being a victim of evil thoughts. Replace every negative thought with a positive one. Be your own game-changer. Enrich your heart with the seeds of positivity, goodness and happiness.

6. Don't cry over petty things. If a situation challenges your beliefs, understand that life is trying to teach you something. And don't fear change as and when required; be wiser and less wrong every new day. Stand for what is right. Believe that what you focus on, you get. Focus on positive thoughts for positive outcomes, feed good words to your mind. Life is full of ups and downs but at least let optimism bring peace to your mind and soul. Stay kind, stay tough.

7. To make others believe in you, you need to first believe in yourselves. Get serious about your goals and see how you shall create an aura of smart people around you. Give out positive energy (to attract more of it) because that's how you make your life wonderful.

GOODWILL

Be a blessing for someone
Help them in healing
Give them wings to fly
And experience the joy of giving

Don't hide your magic
The world needs your light
Do the universe a favour
Help people shine bright

How goodwill helps us to evolve

What counts in goodwill:-

- To bring a smile on someone's face (for making them happy)
- When you lend a helping hand
- Being kind and empathetic towards others
- Being someone's support system (by always staying by their side)
- Donating for charity
- Doing some kind of social work
- Helping someone in healing
- Caring for someone's need
- Fulfilling a promise
- Sharing our blessings
- Performing random acts of kindness to brighten up someone's day
- Planning a surprise for a loved one or a close friend
- Fighting for a good cause
- Making children happy by playing with them
- Making elders happy by spending time with them
- Offering someone help for their work

For me, goodwill means to see good in people and to have a strong faith that goodness can erase any evil. I believe everyone has some goodness in them. Goodwill has helped me survive the most challenging times of my life. At a certain point in my time of depression, I felt like everyone who came close to me had to hurt me, when it was my own demons. Later, I also realized that it was over-care and over-protection of my family that they were taking me to so many doctors and were trying to know what was going in my mind only so that they could help me find the cause behind my disorder. Goodwill brought peace to my mind at such times when I thought that everyone would want me to grow only. Later, I also realized that there is nothing evil in our lives; it's our mind that sometimes cooks up negative stories so that it can remain on the safe side and so that it does not have to use much energy which goes into thinking positive. Sometimes, we are fighting our demons and blame others for whatever happens. This is the way misunderstandings grow and make things even worst or complicated than they are. Sometimes, it's essential to communicate what we feel so that we can avoid conflicts and live peacefully.

Messages to conclude:-

1. We are such a small part of this universe, but we are unique, and that's where we have the power to create a change !!

2. Most of the times, what matters to bring about a change is how many lives we can touch, how many lives we can influence in positive ways, and in how many lives we can make an impact that proves to be helpful for individuals.

3. Aim high. Smile often. Love everyone. Work hard. Laugh often. Feel things. Dream big. Share blessings.

4. Most of the times, our difficult situations come to shape us so that they can lead us to a path where we can follow a purpose so that other people do not have to go through the same pain that we went through and that's how we practice goodwill.

GROWTH

Rise and shine
Blossom like a flower
Take some real efforts
And enjoy the fruits of labour

Leave your comfort zone
Have patience and faith —
Everyone wants you to grow
Inhale positivity with every breath

How I never left growth

Whenever I feel low, I deliberately try to smile so that I can make myself feel good to make things work out. Whenever I start getting any doubts, I try to convince myself that even if anything goes wrong, I'll learn from it, which would ultimately help me to grow. Whenever I am unable to figure out the reason behind certain things, I start thinking positive thoughts to make my faith greater than any doubt/fear. I also believe we should not compare ourselves with others because every individual has a very different and unique journey/story. Instead, we can try our best to set the bar high and break our own records by being better every new day. We should have no resentment towards anyone in life as all the negative feelings hinder our growth only. Whenever you feel disturbed, just close your eyes for a few minutes in meditation and imagine the most beautiful scenes from your dreams and see how all your worries will begin to vanish away. Staying calm in problematic/difficult situations gives our mind time to become clear with the scenario so that it can come up with apt/suitable solutions. Think positive and healing thoughts to fill your mind with grace. Always keep faith believing that things will get right, no matter how tough the path seems at a certain point. Keeping faith not only helps to keep worries away but also helps in healing and growth.

Messages to conclude:-

1. Seize the opportunities life gives you every minute to think positive and shine bright.

2. We all need to practice when to come back in our comfort zone after we have tried staying out of it.

3. Make mistakes. Be better. Work it out. Be confident. Focus better.

4. Make unfamiliar familiar, get comfortable with the uncomfortable and see your life shifting its dimension to the highest form of happiness.

5. Don't wait for opportunities to be a good person. Every new day is a chance to get better and inculcate good habits. Prepare yourself and leave no stone unturned to be your best every day.

6. Growth happens out of the comfort zone only because only when challenges come, we get to understand more about ourselves. Also, we get to realize/learn what values we can hold on as our strengths in different situations.

7. In moments when we feel uncomfortable or when we are out of our comfort zones, we always try our best to make ourselves feel secure (because secure makes us feel safe and happy) and hence growth happens. In the process, we also discover different kind of moments which make us feel peaceful.

8. As long as growth is concerned, you can always experiment in your domain/chosen field.

GREATNESS

Living for others
Making them happy
To love unconditionally —
Promote compassion and empathy

Appreciate great friends
Be cooperative genuinely
Make yourself proud
Choose your battles wisely

Learning to practice greatness

A person becomes great by his deeds, deeds which can provide help to someone. A great person is a giver who keeps contributing to society for its well-being. A great person is one who takes care of everyone around him.

We can always learn to perform little random acts of kindness to spread smiles among our loved ones. Greatness is also shown in the consistent actions when one stays committed to their promises. Greatness is when you fight for a cause and spread happiness among people. Greatness is having team spirit to provide the necessary support to your teammates. Greatness is also seen when one loves a person unconditionally without any expectations in return. A person is great when he promotes compassion, empathy and equality. A person becomes great when he never gives up on his love for his country and so keeps contributing to the society in one or the other way. A great person will share his blessings and he'll be happy by seeing others happy. A great person is the reason that people believe in the goodness of other people because a great person is aware that we should see the good in everything and everyone and stay true to our values. A great person practices kindness and goodwill and makes sure that everyone around him stays happy. A person who tries his best to take away all your sorrows by sharing them so that you don't have to face them alone is a great person. A person who takes care of a friend by treating him equal to a family member is a great person.

Greatness is seen when you respect everyone equally (without any kind of discrimination) and understand that sometimes one needs to make some sacrifices to achieve great things in life. Following your goals and dreams with full passion also makes you great because you might be aware that every responsible citizen of the country adds to its prosperity. We must understand that when each and every citizen on the Earth will play his/her role of life with full sincerity, nothing will be able to stop our planet from flourishing in all the best and extraordinary ways.

Messages to conclude:-

1. Never change yourself for anyone. Be yourself; be terrific. Just evolve, never transform.

2. Smile through the tears, make yourself happy. Use setbacks as stepping stones; make yourself proud.

3. Make this affirmation: I am in the making now for what I want to become and when I shall become, I will again be in the making.

4. Appreciate great friends, support their ideas/opinions, be cooperative genuinely and promote compassion and empathy.

5. Put others before you. Make people happy. Train your mind to see good in everything and everyone. Spread happiness around you.

6. Be passionate for all the things you choose to love in life.

ENERGY

The spirit in you
The fire within —
To work for your dreams
It's the time you begin

You have the zeal
Just vibrate higher
Attract positivity —
Let your life be an adventure

How positive energy and good vibe makes one great

Set goals that can light up energy in you. Give out positive energy so that your aura becomes lively. Whenever you feel dull, try listening to inspirational songs (songs that light up a fire in you), read stories of successful people, share a few words with a stranger and try to cheer yourself up. Think about that feeling of fulfilment of a dream, listen to that voice in your heart that says hard work pays off and never give up on your dreams. Even when it comes to taking small efforts, motivate yourself to do your best because little things when done with full vigour add vitality/liveliness to our moments. Make yourself understand the importance of your role/purpose in life. Try new experiments or hobbies that can fill you with energy because that would also help you to use the creativity of your mind. Only when we try out new things, we allow ourselves to discover hidden talent in us. When it comes to following our passion, we know we'll carry out our tasks with full honesty, but apart from pursuing what we are good at, we can also try things that we think light up a spark in us. Be your best version so that you can use your full potential to contribute to be an asset for the country and inspire people around you to do the same.

Messages to conclude:-

1. Your dreams need you more than you need them. Keep reminding yourself about your purpose.

2. Keep going like a clock. Let it remind you that you have to keep going like you are unstoppable. Keep going despite adversities. The power lies inside you. Use your energy wisely.

3. Expand your horizons, add to your experiences, shake your life a bit, let it be adventurous.

4. Challenge/promise yourself :
   The more something tries to drag me down, the more I'm going to rise with double speed.

5. Work in smart ways, build confidence, strive for greatness and excellence, let your actions reflect your true energy and vibe.

6. Start now, start small but start, make increments every day, all the efforts will add up one day and you'll look back and be proud of yourself that you believed in your ideas more than anyone. If nothing, at least you'll have tried pursuing your passion and not giving up on what you really love doing.

7. Practice your work unless you reach a level of satisfaction that no one could ever match you in your profession.

AWARENESS

To awaken your mind
Understand the situation
To make an impact
Spread light in every direction

Know your strengths
Have consciousness
Share your experience —
Keep spreading awareness

Purpose of spreading awareness

From an education point of view, awareness means to spread the wealth of knowledge that we have regarding different issues. Spreading awareness not only allows us to communicate our thoughts (or express ourselves) but also to enlighten/awaken minds and nurture lives of people around us which ultimately helps in the social and cultural development of a country. Awareness also includes working for a cause to make a positive impact on society. We must understand that it is each and every person's responsibility to care for sustainable development and smooth functioning of a country. If we choose goodwill and unity, every citizen can live a peaceful life. Issues like racial discrimination, human trafficking and problems related to mental health etc should be addressed more frequently so that every individual can gain enough confidence to talk about themselves more openly (without any hesitation). We all can spread awareness by organizing different campaigns in our societies that could deal with simple day-to-day problems so that our joint efforts would let us simplify things for each other. We can learn to volunteer through different workshops, and we must realize that we do have the power to influence people by our optimism. We too can take significant decisions for the welfare of our associations. Many methods can be carried out to spread awareness regarding different issues only if we come together and show some zeal in life.

Self-awareness is when we begin to realize the difference between our conscious and subconscious thoughts and take actions explicitly to better ourselves accordingly. Once we start to observe ourselves, it becomes easy to check/identify which habits need to be changed and what steps could be taken to help and support our friends and family so that everyone can be their best version (to prove an asset to serve the country).

Messages to conclude:-

1. Sit with your feelings once in a while. Talk to yourself positively about things going around you, and somewhere in between, you'll find your peace, comfort and joy.

2. It's necessary that we break the stigmas for different ways in which we live, love and laugh. Let's all educate our instincts so that we can make this world a better place to live in.

3. Rather than judging people upon their opinions, we must understand them because it's always an equal chance for us to make ourselves more aware of how we can spread love.

4. Whenever you feel low, try to recall happy memories, remember/believe that you always have the power to choose your mood, take time to understand your feelings and cheer yourself up. Being gentle with your growth process will always help you in deeper self-awareness.

CELEBRATION

Collect happy moments
Celebrate life
Being alive is the very reason
To enjoy every season

Small steps and small efforts
Bring huge success
Gratitude and good health
Counts for biggest wealth

Life is a beautiful journey to embrace it all

When it comes to family, especially when you have a joint family, a celebration is so much fun. While we celebrate on birthdays, festivals or any occasion, all the cousins gather at one place and enjoy the precious moments while making beautiful memories at the same time. We click pictures, make sweets and special dishes, share our blessings, and this is the way we spread magic at each and every event. Happiness multiplies when we share jokes with each other. We play games and exchange gifts to fill the entire scenario with treasure, excitement and entertainment. The joy that we gain is beyond happiness. Every such experience takes away all our worries/ stress and what remains is the cheerfulness in our hearts and smiles on our faces.

When it comes to friends, especially when you have a crazy circle, celebrating becomes a lot more fun than what we plan. There are surprises on birthdays and more of such happy moments on all of our special days which bring an altogether different feeling of satisfaction to our spirits. The ecstasy we share becomes a fond memory to cherish later. Nostalgic moments that we create add magic to our lives. This makes us realize that the aura is always incredible with our loved ones.

Messages to conclude:-

1. Never miss out on anything that makes you smile. Today even if you pull yourself out of a dark situation, that's also a success.

2. Believe in the fact that small steps and small efforts will bring you huge success one day. You just have to move ahead with all the courage and faith collectively.

3. In your break time, distract yourself with all the right kind of things (that enhance your creativity) so that you can get your understanding of how to enjoy the good things (that are meant for you) in life.

COURAGE

To keep moving forward
Look at the bright side
To face adversities
Have faith in your abilities

Do not fear change;
To be extraordinary —
Acknowledge your feelings;
For each wound has got teachings

When you choose to be courageous, how it creates wonders

What is courage?

Practical examples of moments in which an individual exhibits courage:-

- When you know that you have to fight the same demons over and over, but you do not quit
- When you choose to be brave at your weakest by reminding yourself of all your values and blessings
- When you follow your principles, you are aware of the fact that you have the power to make certain things possible by giving in all your efforts.
- When you choose to stay out of your comfort zone to try out new things such that it might help you or someone else to grow
- When you fight for your rights and a peaceful life
- When you decide to stay strong in tough times
- When you keep your faith bigger than the doubts
- When you push/motivate yourself to achieve great things in life
- When you decide not to give up on your passion
- When you decide to stay calm and just focus on your growth
- When you pick yourself up after a long fight with your anxiety
- When you pull yourself out of a dark situation
- When you are being your own light (helping yourself along your journey)
- When you work hard and stay strong for someone
- When you love someone unconditionally

- When you break the stigmas for different ways of living
- When you don't let setbacks, hurdles, challenges or tough times to stop you from achieving your dreams
- When you choose to stay strong for your parents and loved ones
- When you choose to change your perspective during challenging times
- When you push yourself a little more than yesterday for a better today
- When you are aware that the limits that exist in your mind can be extended and won over one by one so that there are no more limits, only love would exist
- When you are bold enough to follow your heart keeping in mind what's best for your spirit (it takes practice to choose what's best for us)
- When you can forgive someone special infinite times
- When you fight hard to make someone proud of you
- When you dream of being an inspiration for people
- When you cheer yourself up to overcome a tough situation/challenge and then choose to share your blessings

Messages to conclude:-

1. Look at the bright side, let perspective shift and faith (in one's spirit) be your guiding light.

2. Never fear walking on a different path. Sometimes when you don't get any signs, just believe in your heart and make your faith bigger than the fear. It requires immense courage to run your own race. Be your own light.
   No crisis is too hot for you to survive.

3. Keep trying new things, believe in your beliefs but don't fear change because the only thing that keeps us going is change. Advancement is key.

4. To accomplish your goals, let there be sheer perseverance running in your nerves. We all just need an absolute kind of awakening to realize our real power. Challenge yourself every single day to be better than yesterday.

5. Have faith in yourself, have faith in your abilities, have faith in the process, have faith in your journey, have faith in positive energy, have faith in good vibes, have faith in magic, have faith in miracles, have faith in the universe.

6. It takes a great deal of courage to share your vulnerability that comes with enduring and accepting things while we learn to grow through it all.

7. It's you who gets to define your bravery every time you decide to work hard for the things you love.

JOURNEY INSIDE

Is it a need or desire
Or is it an instinct
To which I'm adding some reality

Is it a part of my dream
Or is it some inner wish
That my heart is making

Is it my love for the nation
Or just a simple call
To fulfil a duty

I could ask myself
To analyze
What is it?

How actions build your dreams

For every word in our mind, there's a feeling associated if it's good or bad. When we feed good words and good thoughts, our mind releases happiness hormones. On the other side, negative words degrade our thought pattern. Hence, we must allow only the very best information to enter our minds. Only sometimes, it's fair to experience the bad to appreciate the good fully.

We must question our actions, whether they are fruitful for our growth or not. To achieve a better understanding of our thought pattern, we must be open to new ideas and allow ourselves to feel what our heart wants to follow. At the same time, we can sometimes simply educate our instincts when we think they need to be guided in the right direction.

Our subconscious mind often follows a pattern because of which we generalize things and build boundaries so that we can save ourselves from any harm. Instead, we must allow ourselves to embrace the good and endure the bad so that we can give life its true meaning and let faith gain victory over our fears.

My chachu taught me how one could focus on their needs and not on their desires because your desires feed your ego. He also taught me that if once we learn to live through our actions, it would be then when we would not live from our mind but our soul power. When we'll keep taking actions, we would not have to think much about our thoughts, and we will keep performing things which would ultimately help us to achieve our every dream.

Messages to conclude:-

1. Your desires satisfy your ego. Always ask yourself whether you are listening to your needs or your desires.

2. Take responsibility for your actions, only that shall make you free.

3. Study yourself, and you will be able to find all the motivation inside that you were trying to search outside all this while.

4. Decide for yourself which event you would like to keep a possibility (educate your instinct) and which one you would convert into reality (follow your instinct).

5. Spirituality is to follow what you preach. Spirituality is working on oneself. It's to take responsibility for our own actions and to be aware of the fact that we all are unique in our own beautiful ways.

6. Never suppress your instinct (a tiny voice from the heart) and intuition (a small voice in head) because that's the spark that makes you truly unique.

7. Unless a habit is formed, we need to take actions explicitly which is done through our conscious part of the mind. Once we learn and master a particular thing, it becomes a part of our subconscious mind. That's the reason why we need to try and practice stuff till they can become a part of us, till they can add to our skills and capabilities and till we can achieve excellence in them.

HELP FOR GOODWILL

How do I help myself
Do I take support
'Coz they say it's courageous

How do I do it
Am I self-reliant
Or learning to trust with boundaries

How do I become my guiding light
Do I care much
So I could team up

Or am I wise enough
To imagine my future version
Then helping myself wisely.

Question of asking for help always ponders

Some people are not good at asking for help because, throughout their lives, they have learnt self-reliance. Sometimes, it depends on our upbringing that how we have been brought up to adopt certain values.

It's about April 2020 when again I had started to show symptoms of insomnia after its treatment in January 2020 (I was on medication for about two years). While I was thinking certain thoughts and wondering to find answers to different questions (all sorts of questions about universe), I think some negative thoughts too entered my mind which might have been the reason behind my relapse. After three days of continuous overthinking (with very little sleep), I could not stop my flow of thoughts and had to take help from someone. I had read it online in one of the posts of Harrdy Sandhu (a very famous cricketer, actor and singer) that nothing is more artistic than loving people. When I recalled it suddenly somewhere from my memory, that's when I paused for a moment and gave a thought to it and went to call my mother to sleep with me for a night. That whole night, I went for vomiting 5-6 times, but as my mom was there to provide me with the necessary help just so I could feel better, I felt secure. That day I decided that I wanted to make her win. She has suffered a lot for me. She is so strong that seeing her now, I wish to have that much strength in my life. She has seen me grow while I fought all my battles, and all the while, she has been so patient with me. She deserves all the happiness, peace and blessings such that I can make her feel proud to have raised a strong/brave daughter.

After this incident of overthinking, I kind of felt "brainwashed". Also, this might be the reason behind a symptom observed later in which I had difficulty in memorizing things. Just some negative thoughts (due to some content consumed online) and my medication again started.

One thing that I learnt from all this is that we should keep spreading smiles and good vibes. You never know who might be suffering alone. We must keep offering help to people around us so that everyone feels loved and stays happy.

Messages to conclude:-

1. Love your dear ones beyond imperfections, embrace their flaws, support them, give them wings to fly, live for goodwill and keep spreading smiles.

FLY FREE

And when I run to share it with you
All my happy moments
What is this feeling?

I know it shall become memorable
So I live it to the fullest
And try to hold onto it

It multiplies the madness
As we slowly add our magic
To make it heavenly

Our efforts decorate it
Beyond eternity
What is this magical feel?

Sharing stories and blessings

There are some moments in life which make you feel loved and special and all such moments are magical in their own beautiful ways, for example: listening to your favourite song on repeat, going on a long drive with someone special, celebrating little moments of happiness, a dream come true feeling, when you meet your best friend after a long break, when you observe extraordinary miracles in nature etc. Such moments when shared with your loved ones, add beauty to your story. The vibes that we spread while sharing our blessings bring ecstasy all around; such is the power of love that we carry within our hearts. When you have someone by your side to support you through your journey, it becomes easy to fight your battles of life as you are aware that gratitude envelopes/protects you and also you automatically get the strength needed to fight with your struggles. When we share our feelings with someone, it not only acts as a means to spread love, but we can also learn new ways to follow the principles of unity, teamwork, compassion and goodwill. Good times are always awaited/cherished when we have to wait for a long time for some special occasion to arrive. Making memories and all such happy moments bring liveliness to our hearts. Our heart dances with joy when we share smiles with someone because sharing things makes us feel loved and blessed.

Messages to conclude:-

1. Spread smiles and good vibes.

FRIENDSHIP NOSTALGIA (HAPPY MEMORIES)

Those were the days
Of endless conversations
Togetherness, our passion
Being crazy, our only hobby

Laughing out loud
Our most beautiful therapy
Limitless craziness
And all the happy memories

Sharing secrets
How we build a beautiful bond,
Wonderful people for life
Give support and warmth

Friends like family
Tease all along —
Our ways add magic
Infinite happiness we cherish !!

Finding a true friend
With the same mindset
Gives thrill and excitement
With an added flavour of thankfulness

Singing and dancing together
Learned our lessons
Through laughter and tears —
We could call it our most beautiful decade

Little hearts
Hope to re-live and re-create
Times of eternal joy
And the most happy days

Love-lessons from friends,
That our cheating in exams,
That our going to movies
Bunking classes and all the fun

Surprises for birthdays,
Contributions to buy the gifts
Making everyone feel special,
How do we re-create those memories !!

Giving innovative solutions
To make people around
Forget all their problems —
To care for all those smiles

Clicking pictures in every corner
From sharing every moment —
How has it all turned
To making each other proud

School, college and office mates
Made plans and cancelled
The way we grow together
To blame it all on the system

Little things and simple pleasures
Those rides and our night out
Still thinking of each other
Connecting dots and bridges

Thankful for all the support
For all those who come in life —
We feel loved and blessed
To have lived a dream like life.

How friends add colour to life

A NOSTALGIC BOND (As written for my relationship with my best friend when we were in college)

Togetherness is our passion, being crazy is our hobby, loving each other is our favourite past time and laughing out loud is what all we need. And yes, we are the ones who have given a new dimension to the term "friendship" in our own way. After the first meet, it's like we are in the same shoe, and since then, our conversation is endless, and our craziness is limitless. We never need to second guess, whether to reveal our secrets to one another. We never miss a chance to laugh out loud and not stop until our jaws start paining or we have a sudden ache in our stomach. Meeting each other after a long break multiplies our madness and our excitement to see each other won't stop until we share what all happened in our vacations. What's fantastic is that we always appreciate our being so weird and insane. If one of us cries, the other one, no doubt, will start talking senseless and will do all the drama to make the partner forget all the problems. We will do all the nuisance by teasing each other in the mid of a lecture, by singing and dancing in the corridor when no one's around us, by finding ways to see each other and the list is never-ending.

I had written the above lines when we (I and my best friend) were in college. Isn't it that we miss our school and college life so much that we wish we could go back in time and re-live those moments we cherished together !!

Messages to conclude:-

1. The times we remember the most in our lives are the times when we had to adjust and struggle, and when we celebrated and laughed till our cheeks started to pain.

2. Friends make for the most beautiful colours in painting the canvas of gratitude in life.

DANCER COUSIN

The way your eyes express
Pure magic and twinkle
Those moves sync with the music
When you perform with the perfect twist

Sharp stance and dynamic dance
The way you hold and balance,
With a smile that connects,
Heartfelt expressions are also bright !!

What a treat to eyes
To watch you create
Your epic steps of madness
Hit and rock the floor every-time!

What co-ordination of hands and feet
The way you interact with music
How do you do it so perfectly!
With superb presence of mind

Timing, feel and energy
Makes the aura awesome
With love-filled grace
Your acts look simply effortless.

When I met my crazy cousin

An inspiring story of a cousin, who is a very great dancer, has held me by surprise. His name is Karan and what I have observed about him is that he dances very gracefully. When I saw his videos, which he keeps posting on different social media platforms, I became curious about how did he perform so magically.

When he was in 5th or 6th standard, he danced in front of his class, but everyone started laughing. Not only this but when he performed in school functions also, he was made to stand behind other dancers. One day, when there was someone's marriage at his house, he got inspired to choose to learn dance when he saw a relative of his doing handstand. After a series of events that inspired him to become a dancer, he had decided that he wanted to become a great dancer. When in 8th or 9th standard, he wanted to join a dance class, he did not get enough support from his family. So, he collected some pocket money to pay his fees for dance class and then later started one to teach dance. He had to face endless struggles along his journey to become a successful choreographer. He went in different reality shows like Dance India Dance (season 4) and India's Dancing Superstar for giving auditions and even got selected in top 200 contestants which is itself a big victory. He used to watch videos of dance instructors on YouTube and had a dream to learn from an international artist. Somehow, he got a chance to meet that artist, and his dream came true. He wanted to join Urban Dance Camp in the US. For the same, he searched their website but unfortunately, due to high expenses, he could not afford to go there. Now he keeps posting his dance videos on Facebook, Instagram, YouTube and Moj etc.

Simultaneously, he attends dance workshops and also keeps winning battles in various competitions.

He also went to Mumbai for the audition of India's Got Talent which made him learn about different struggles of life. He had to face many rejections before he could get proper direction in life. He has been practising dance since years, and he's also taken training in it. He used to travel a lot to different cities to learn from different masters. Every learning added to his experience, and finally, in 2019, he got many achievements. He's also got a job offer from Singapore and is planning to go there to spread his magic. He is inspired from every little thing to create his dance moves and believes in showcasing his talent in his unique style so that he can connect with people in a very pure way (a way that touches the heart). Many artists have shared his videos online during these times of pandemic. He believes his every video, and every struggle is a different story that has not only made him learn different lessons but also has helped him grow incredibly through his journey.

He loves the way music is created and how steps are formed on different beats. He keeps trying new experiments with body isolations and musicality. For him, the feel and the happiness that he gets from dancing is way more important than simply dancing to make videos. He keeps adding things to dance to master the art form in all the perfect ways. According to him, the definition of dance means to move on the music. So, whenever he dances, he keeps this in mind that his moves should come straight from the heart. He says he can dance on any new piece of music which he might not have even heard before. He loves challenges and is growing better every new day. His parents and his friends try to support him in every way possible. He says that technology has helped a lot of people to come forward to showcase their talent, which was not the case earlier when he started to dance. He is optimistic in believing that despite all the ups and downs, his journey has been full of fun. He keeps getting calls for auditions and has also been posting videos on Moj so that he can inspire more people to dance and stay fit.

Messages to conclude:-

1. From thinking and dreaming about it to start taking action, it makes all the difference.

2. Magic happens when you don't give up. Keep trying at that which gets your heart elated.

IDENTITY

They say change yourself
Not only this, in fact,
You have to be the change
It doesn't end here, to add,
They say 'adjust the sail'
And change your perspective
There's more to share,
They say advancement is the key
In an ever-changing world;
Could you define 'change'
Could you define 'identity'
So now who knows
What's the definition of 'acceptance'
There's a whole list to it
Evolve, transform,
Be yourself, be terrific,
Be your best version,
Believe in your beliefs,
Develop a new mindset;
Now it feels like
All the answers are hidden
And you have to find the secret
That goes for you.
It's a long journey to explore
Journey inside might help,
One shall study their heart,
With a touch of madness
It shall all lead us,
Drive us all
To our best fit
And our most happy place.

There are so many rules out there, what to accept and what not !!

Sometimes, we feel we have to keep changing our behaviour according to our surroundings so that we can fit in such that people accept us. It happens that whenever we try to be ourselves, some people start thinking that we are weird and the others will feel that we act in strange ways. They think so because they look at things through a very narrow perception. It is us who must understand that we should not take everything personally. There are our loved ones to care for us, and so only their opinions should matter to us. We should be aware of the fact that good people only push us to grow when they believe in our capabilities. When someone is strict with us, it only means that they want us to be the best. One must have no ill will towards anyone in life because the people who are rude to you need the most kindness and light so that they can learn to spread genuine love among everyone. It is our choices that decide who we become in life. When circumstances are not in our control, we must be aware and remember that at least we have an option to hold onto hope and optimism, which surely would help us to tackle our problems in better ways.

When we allow others to define our identity by considering their negative comments, we not only give them power/ control over us but also let them assume that we aren't a proper fit for the society or for the kind of the world that they have created in their mind. We must be brave enough to let go of the negativity to make way for all that is positive in this world. Sometimes, we need to change our perspective for certain things in life that we believe could help us to improve our understanding of things and the other times we can just embrace it all not because we wish to satisfy ourselves but to learn to accept our spirit and mind for all that it offers.

Messages to conclude:-

1. If you are going in the right direction, one day you'll be surprised at the fact that what you are doing is magical. Don't give up and be so perfect in your work that nobody else can do it your way.

2. Be such a sincere soul that you can set a practical example of an inspirational being for people around you.

3. Never let your worth depend on other people's validation of who you are. Celebrate little progress that you keep making every-time while marching to your destination.

4. Never change how you show love. Don't lose yourself (the real you) just for the sake of someone's acceptance criteria. Be authentic, be genuine.

5. The day you sow the seeds is not the day you get fruits. Similarly, the development of any seed (love or optimism, etc.) within our heart takes time to show results. It takes an extreme degree of practice, patience and persistence throughout the process. You can win through it all and emerge with an essence/fragrance of beauty to create the aura of love, happiness and positivity.

6. Give yourself timeline only if you work well under pressure and if you don't, just let yourself flow with life and do what your heart says.

7. One needs to put unbelievable efforts to become an irreplaceable spirit.

8. Life is what we take it to be. Have the mindset of a legend.

FIRE

Let there be wounds
Let there be growth
Go where your soul rises,
Let your heart guide you
Let it show you the way
Let it take you
To all the dark places
To fill you with grace
And to discover
What's still left
For the world to see.
Help yourself,
Stand for yourself
You can do it,
You've got this
Life is a challenge
Be tough, be kind
Let yourself flow freely
Drink all the passion
And ignite the spark
For now is the time
To fly away
With your dreams.
You see it's dark everywhere
May be the light
Is coming from you
Hope for optimism
Dance through your struggles,
Let your journey heal you,
Let the storms open your heart,
Let hope win today.

Follow the spark in you

Sometimes, we don't get answers to few questions, we don't understand why things are the way they are, we can't find sense/logic/reason behind certain things, but even in such situations, there is hope. We can always choose to rise while realizing that we already have the strength needed to get back up every time we face a setback, no matter how many of them try to pull us down. Sometimes, it's the messiest/chaotic days that make us realize about the light/ magic/heaven that lies within us. Only when there's a tough challenge in front of us, we get to understand what qualities we can hold on to such that we can always use them as our weapons while fighting the battles of life. With little patience, faith and magic, everything starts making perfect sense. Little things like the laugh of a child, long conversation with our best friend, sharing our blessings with someone, helping someone with their work or trying a new hobby etc have the power to reinvigorate life in us. There is so much in life to be grateful for, and so it's better to focus on good things. Even in the darkest phase of life, you can discover something so beautiful that the world would congratulate you upon your findings. Believe that there's a point behind every little thing that happens to you, even when you can't find it. It's the tough times that fill us with grace and purpose. We just have to find the truth for all the moments that our heart dreams of achieving. There's a little voice inside each one of us that keeps guiding us to grow only when we know how to observe our deep feelings.

Messages to conclude:-

1. The small pleasures you sacrifice today will make your big dreams come true tomorrow.

2. Wish your dream with all your heart and see how your mind, body and soul will help you achieve it.

3. Live such a life that one day you can tell your story to everyone to bring about a change and to inspire others.

4. Let the fire in you burn so bright that you're able to fight all the battles happily and peacefully. Take one day at a time and let hope win every single day.

LITTLE CHILDREN

Unique flowers of a garden
Bring us huge joy;
Their love is unconditional
Why are they so adorable ?
Their sweet innocence,
Their naughtiness,
Their lovely expressions
Give warmth to your soul.
Their laugh is like
Music in life —
Little bundles of joy
Having twinkle in eyes;
Slowly learn to grow
To become ultimate wonders.
The way they learn
To crawl, to jump, to speak,
To climb the stairs,
And when they learn to express;
Bright spark and hope
They could teach you
To enjoy little moments
To stay happy and content
To not worry.
You would never forget
Their cheerfulness
The way they rise
After every fall.

You would also agree
They give you
Fragrance of childhood
So we all wish
We could be child again.
Their just one smile
Takes away all our sorrows,
Love the way
They ask questions —
Little packets of energy
We all love them, isn't it?

How little bundles of joy create wonders growing up

Little children are truly adorable and full of innocence. They are always full of life and energy. Their naughty smile makes us forget all our worries. They teach us that we should enjoy every little moment as it comes (as life unfolds) and how we can spread unconditional love. They never discriminate us based on age, caste, religion, sex, race or personality. It's us who teach them about differences in life. They are never biased. They are simply pure-hearted. They play a significant role in our lives as they bring so much joy in a family such that the whole house lights up with happiness.

Messages to conclude:-

1. Have curiosity, ask all sorts of questions. Learn things by fun. Choose some hobby that helps you enhance your creativity.

2. Live in the moment. Enjoy every second to the fullest because it counts. Stay happy and positive in every kind of situation. Make memories and new experiences. Keep learning, and have fun.

DEPRESSION

You are not alone
Mental health is important
You practice gratitude
So you can feel loved,
Every-time you have to believe
More than ever,
You have to have faith
That you have the power
To look on the bright side
And be your own master.
Sometimes you feel low
And by the time
You learn to cope up,
You again feel high,
Acknowledge your feelings,
You can choose
To smile in difficult times,
You're such a sport.
Accept, heal and recover
For it is curable —
Just give yourself time,
Be kind and gentle,
And don't give up,
For you can choose
To be positive.
You wish you could
Break the stigma
Of depression,
Anxiety and insomnia —
You are brave.

Allow yourself
To fight with the demons
For it won't last long,
And deep inside you know
You can choose hope,
And take care of yourself.
Stay strong, stay flexible
For this fight is tough;
Cheer yourself up
Let your spirit rise
Let there be
No time for tears
Be your own game-changer
And know this fact
Sometimes it's okay
To feel vulnerable,
You have the willpower
To fight this confusion.
From so long
It has got you stuck
That you don't know
What is normal,
But again you can choose
To awaken the courage
To stay tough
And to survive —
Coz every new day
Is a blessed day
That you're alive
And still choose to rise.

Story of depression and relapse:-
(Mental health and wellness)

March 2018 (first consultation) to January 2020 was the duration for which my disorder lasted. I was diagnosed with insomnia (difficulty falling asleep), anxiety and depression; so the doctor had to start medication. There occurred some kind of chemical imbalance in the brain due to which there was lack of happiness hormones (mainly dopamine and serotonin). Symptoms observed were sleeplessness, crying easily etc.

I remember, in one of my meetings with the doctor, he had advised me to be flexible. So, I use to be gentle with myself and use to acknowledge my feelings. I use to work on it, bit by bit, by replacing negative thoughts with positive ones. It worked for me, fortunately. Doses of medicine kept changing. Obviously, treatment takes time and commitment. The first thing is to accept it. Other measures that we can apply to cure it include:-

Practice gratitude, keep our faith bigger than the fears, go out to take fresh air, make small goals and achieve them (happiness accomplished releases serotonin)

Recovery is full of ups and downs. Never understood the reason behind two things:-

1. Whether I was curing myself by being positive or was it the medicine.
2. The reason behind crying (actually feeling low or just no reason).

But it leaves you strong. Every hardship brings some kind of blessing with it. So, don't give up. BE KIND to everyone. Be the reason someone smiles today.

Story of relapse:-
(Get aware about mental health)

April 2020 is when my medication for the treatment of insomnia, anxiety and depression again started (Previously it lasted from March 2018 to January 2020). Doses of medicine keep changing. October 2020 and I'm still taking medications.

Symptoms observed include:-

- Difficulty falling asleep
- Memory problems (difficulty in memorizing)
- Feeling low (uncertain mood)

Measures being taken for recovery include:-

- Practising gratitude
- Replacing negative thoughts with positive ones
- Looking on the bright side of things
- Being gentle/flexible with the growth process
- Acknowledging feelings
- Following the formula of 'accept, heal and recover' to endure through the bad
- Trying to practice keeping happy
- Keeping faith that it had been cured before, so again it can cure soon

Anyone struggling from any such mental disorder should stay strong, reach out for help, stay flexible and positive, take fresh air, observe their mood pattern and try performing tasks that involve some mental exercise (all these help in the release of happiness hormones).

Messages to conclude:-

1. The more you try to own and hold onto something, the more it slips away from you. Let there be a sense of balance and moderation in all things you do.

2. Take care of your mental health in different ways in which you can cheer yourself up. Practice making and achieving small goals. Keep habits that heal. Using creativity of mind will ultimately help you in some mental exercise, and in the process, you will also learn about how you can keep yourself happy.

3. When we continuously think about future, we become anxious. When we always want to keep ourselves busy, we keep thinking about what to do in the next moment (which builds anxiety), so we aren't able to experience the present moments/emotions fully. We must live in the present moment so that we can enjoy life as it comes (sometimes we need to flow freely). Also, planning things beforehand can help to organize them better.

4. Our failures make us. They give us lessons to learn, they give us opportunities to become better, they give us a chance to correct our mistakes, and they make us wise. Every hardship comes with some kind of blessing, so we must focus on the bright side of things.

5. Fear and worry are the two worst diseases. They make you sick even before you are actually sick.

6. We all need to realize that we are already strong from within and we can always decide/choose to be brave every time a situation challenges us, which would ultimately make us courageous.

STUDENTS AT BLIND SCHOOL

Brave hearts
Live with optimism,
They walk together
Holding hands,
Rise and shine
In mysterious ways.
Every day
They show infinite hope
When they choose
To survive
And not give up
The fight.
They learn and study Braille,
Perceive things differently,
It might be a tough life
For them, still
They smile.
In love with the way
They are so passionate;
Having big dreams,
And amazed with the fact
That they have
So much strength;
Can't see but will feel
The beauty of a good heart,
Will teach you
Helping nature,

To care and share,
And will win your hearts
Simply by their innocence,
They are truly an inspiration;
So, it feels good
To be inspired
From these students
At blind school.

How students at blind school are an inspiration

I teach in a blind school as a social service. It has been a great experience with students there as I've got to learn so much from them. While I've seen them grow, I've got to realize that life is really tough for some people out there. Every single day is a struggle for them. Some of them are partially blind, and the others are fully blind. I think they have to work harder than people who have sight because they have to build their place in this world, which gives equal competition to them. For sure, this disability does not stop them from achieving their dreams. This fighting spirit in them inspires me the most.

I would love to share the experience that I had with them. I think these students at blind school have quite mysterious ways of living life. When they have to move from one place to another, they walk holding each other's hand (taking each other's support). They touch and try to feel things. Their hearing sense is quite good. They are so passionate about life and have such big dreams that this very thing about them surprises me and makes me wonder how are they so strong. Nothing stops them from smiling, laughing big, having fun and enjoying life and this very fact is the reason for their inspiring nature.

An incident that made me speechless one day happened to occur in one of my sessions at class while my students were meditating. When I told a student of mine to close his eyes, he responded that he already could not see, and so how did it matter to close the eyes. I was shocked listening to this, paused for a moment and gave a thought to his answer to politely explain to him that closing eyes helped in concentrating better.

The thing is that the students very well know how to enjoy every little moment. They are always so excited to learn new things. They sing, dance, attend workshops, play games and can also operate phones and computer. Technology has made all the things possible for them. They learn and study Braille, which is a form of written language in which characters are represented by patterns of raised dots that are felt with the fingertips.

These days (in the times of pandemic), they are taught online. We, teachers, voice record our lessons and send them to our students through a social media platform. These students have so much strength in them that I believe that one day they all will succeed in achieving their dreams by facing all the challenges that life has to put in front of them.

Messages to conclude:-

1. Learn lessons from all those experiences the world keeps facing and apply them to your own hardships, and see the majority of problems vanishing from your life.

MY PET DOG

It's all about
My pet dog,
When you touch his tail
He will come
To remove your hand,
Sometimes he climbs
On your bed,
And you have to
Pull him down,
He loves to sleep
On the floor,
He will wag his tail
So that you come
And show some love
To him.
You can hug and kiss him
Whenever you wish,
His warmth is pleasant,
His eyes convey
All his feelings,
He comes running
When you offer him
Food and snacks,
Sits silently waiting for you,
Then again gets up
In sometime
Just to roam
Here and there,
Adorable in his ways
Uses tricks to catch the ball,

Will jump and act innocent
For his food,
In love with his naughtiness
And the way he loves
Unconditionally,
He waits for that
One glance of yours,
For that affection
He waits
When he feels cold and hungry.
What I understand
His message would be
That he doesn't want
To disturb anyone but
He loves it
When we play with him,
Our love is all he needs,
He wants us to be kind
With him,
And he knows
That pets like him
Can at least expect
Some warmth
From all of us.
That's all about
My sweet and lovely
Pet dog.

What message would pets want to convey?

What I understand every pet's message to all the humans out there would be:-

I keep waiting for you so that you come and feed me. I wait for that one glance of yours. I wait for that affection you could show me in times of my hardship. I feel cold and hungry, and can't even express that. I hope you understand that I don't want to disturb you, but I love it when you play with me. Your love is all I need. Every day is a struggle for me because I have to find food for myself. I hope you are aware of this fact and adopt me someday. Be kind and please don't hurt me. I also have only one life like you, and I know I can at least expect some warmth from you.

Messages to conclude:-

1. Unconditional love is love with acceptance and love without expectations. Spread such love.

2. Be kind and gentle with everyone.

RAINFALL

Everything is so mesmerizing
About rainfall,
The music rain creates,
The dewdrops on leaves,
Swift movement of clouds,
The cool breeze,
Thunder and lightning
And that's the way
The monsoon takes
All the stress away.
The smell of mud
A beautiful fragrance,
The way rains bring
Soothing effect on flowers
As the spring awaits
Round the corner,
Dancing of peacock
Opening its feathers,
A mood to rejoice
And get playful
In the rains
Is all one needs
To refresh their spirit.
Birds fly
Even when it rains
So we can learn
This teaching from them
To not give up
Against all odds.

With a little sunshine
The rainbow it creates,
Spreading beauty all around
The aura it creates,
Love everything about rains
The magic it spreads,
Little miracles of nature
Never fail to amaze.

When rainfall takes you into a new world

The way rainfall clears the air, spreads greenery all around and brings freshness teaches us the importance of nourishment and cleanliness. Hope and acceptance can be learnt by the rainfall when it combines with sunshine to form rainbows. When the clouds let go of their heaviness, something refreshing, i.e. rain follows. Similarly, when we let go the dark moments, we make space for something beautiful and refreshing to be followed in our lives.

Messages to conclude:-

1. There is a process for everything in nature like the water cycle, sea breeze, land breeze; all these cycles keep nature in harmony. Similarly, we should learn to keep our mind, body, heart n soul in harmony.

2. Humans should clean and purify their thoughts, just like nature takes care of itself.

A TRIBUTE TO NATURE

Nature song

The rivers and the waterfall
The flowers and the plants
Landscape and air
Around us, everywhere

A sky so wide
To reach that height
Birds and animals
Also roaming, insects and mammals

The snow on the mountains
The dark clouds
Raindrops falling on you
Take you to another world, so new!

A gift to mankind
The hills and the valleys
Miracles of mother nature
Spread fragrance in air

Let's learn from them
The unstoppable flow
Like water in seas
And a forest of trees

The moon and the stars
Sunrise and sunset
Trees so tall
Let's save them all.

How little miracles of nature can inspire an individual

There are endless lessons one can learn by observing nature. It seems as if nature receives powers from some magical force and then showers the blessings to the whole world.

Trees teach inner power. They teach us to stand tall and firm, no matter what. They make us learn how to bear storms in life. The way they teach us how to use our inner power to achieve tremendous strength is also unbelievable. They are a perfect combination of vulnerability and strength. Even Earth, as a whole, bearing the weight of nature and humans, teaches us strength. Birds and animals when go out in the world every single day in search of food and water, they teach us strength. Mountains standing tall and firm teach us to be robust and proud. The sand on the beaches as it bears the scorching heat of the sun teaches us strength. The moon and the stars light up the whole universe when it's dark. They teach us that little darkness is required to see the shine and sparkle we possess. Birds, as they come together to build their homes, teach us unity. A butterfly is a perfect example to learn hope, grace and patience. The way a caterpillar turns into a butterfly teaches us to trust in our growth process and to enjoy it. The way flowers grow with poise and slowly get their colours teaches us grace. The way water in the lakes, ponds, rivers, seas, and waterfall regulates itself through water cycle teaches us the importance of purity and cleanliness.

All the lessons learnt from nature can be applied in real life to achieve heights and overall excellence.

Messages to conclude:-

1. Sky gives a platform to sun, moon and stars so that they can shine at their own times. Similarly, life is a platform to live (perform/present/showcase/write/create) your best story.

2. Like the trees smile in the sunshine, the way they hold so many branches together, in a similar way, my dear you have the power to hold on to your strengths, and smile in difficult situations. With the infinite love that you carry in your heart, you shall overcome the impossible one day.

3. Nature is the biggest healer and the best therapy. It helps you build strength. It is the best example to remind us to just focus on our growth and stay calm during the storms of life.

4. As mother nature does, accept every phase of life with open arms. Fill your soul with grace and positivity.

ABOUT THE AUTHOR

Nitu Ramchandani is a warm-hearted personality. She believes that goodwill is the purest form of love. She is always inspired by teachings and words of Madhuri Dixit, a great idol and a huge inspiration.

Nitu loves simple living and high thinking. When her experiences married her research, she found interest in expressing her thoughts and emotions through different poems. It's her dream to become a great poet, writer and author. Nitu loves to explore various things, things that can add meaning to her life.

You may connect with Nitu through her Facebook page – Library of a poet (facebook.com/Libraryofapoet) or Instagram page (https://instagram.com/libraryofapoet)